STEP INTO THE MEADOW

*A Year in the Life of
a Dales Meadow*

Words and pictures by
Judith Bromley

SMITH SETTLE
1996

First published in 1996 by
Smith Settle Limited
Ilkley Road
Otley

ISBN   Paperback   1 85825 062 5
        Hardback   1 85825 063 3
        Special   1 85825 064 1

Printed and bound by
Smith Settle
Ilkley Road   Otley   LS21 3JP

CONTENTS

ACKNOWLEDGEMENTS

There are a great number of people I would like to thank, too many to name
them all, but amongst these are the following:

Mr & Mrs Tennant for allowing me to walk off the
footpath and sit carefully in their field to paint

Charles Kightly; Joyce Entwhistle; Alice Hodgson;
and Liz, Mandy, Ben and Sarah from the Nature Conservancy
Council for their help in the preparation of this book

For their active help and in pursuing lines of enquiry
my cousin Mary, David Green, Jo Scott, David Baker,
and Kath & Bill Hird

David Bellamy for his enthusiasm in the early stages, and to
David Joy, Roger Chapman, Lord Peel, and Tim Holman at
several stages along the way

All my family and friends for their ongoing interest,
support and encouragement, much needed at times,
especially Deborah Millward for her 'behind the scenes'
positive assistance

and to Ken Smith at Smith Settle for his generosity in
making this book possible. There have been two voices at
the end of the telephone which I shall always remember.
Alison at YWT and Tracey at Smith Settle — both always
helpful and considerate

Last but not least my thanks to Nik for the gift of two
drawings for my book.

I would like to dedicate this book to my parents:
in memory of my father,
and in celebration of my mother's 90th birthday.

PUBLISHER'S ACKNOWLEDGEMENTS

The publisher would like to acknowledge with
grateful thanks the following individuals
and companies who have supported
this publication:

The Contributors

Lord Peel   Robert Hardy
David Bellamy   Judi Dench
Betty Boothroyd   Geoff Boycott
Victoria Wood   Alan Bennett

———————

Keith Bromley

Michael Bromley

Peter Bromley at Russell and Bromley Ltd

Mr & Mrs Petty

Dr & Mrs Alder

Sue Holden

———————

Studio North Limited
(colour separations)

MCImaging Limited
♣ Mitsubishi Corporation
(film and plates)

Rothera and Brereton Limited
 (paper)

Introduction

I have lived most of my life in the Dales, and have spent half my time wishing I wasn't about to leave, and the other half wishing I was back.

Like all rural areas the Yorkshire Dales have their own identity and characteristics. Some of these have doggedly hung on, despite the inevitability of change, whereas others have buckled under the economic pressure for survival.

The Dales have many features, but perhaps the most distinct is that almost symbiotic relationship that exists between the grey barns and the stone walls which seem to stem from them, and that subtle mix of colours of the meadow land which they protect. Rich in herbs, insects and birds, the hay meadows of the Yorkshire Dales are surely one of natures greatest creations.

As with so many landscapes, their nature conservation value has deteriorated since the war. This has occurred largely on the back of a desire for easily available and cheap food, combined with the political will to support the Hill Farmer.

Admirable though these objectives are, a balance needs to be struck, and fortunately changes are now happening. Present Government policy reflects the strong desire by so many to conserve the most threatened and important habitats, and the hay meadows are among a list of such habitats which now benefit from special protection. This, combined with the effort of voluntary conservation organisations, like the Yorkshire Wildlife Trust, and certain individuals, has seen a renaissance in the well-being of the hay meadow.

However despite this welcome change it is estimated that there are now only 5,000 hectares remaining in Great Britain, the majority of which exist in the Dales and the Lake District. Elsewhere in the world only Greenland, Norway and Sweden include such habitats. The plant community, which is found in the Dales meadows, is thought to be directly descended from the plant community that existed in clearings within the wildwood that developed after the ice age. The individual species themselves are not particularly rare, but as a community they are indeed special, and worthy of great attention. The work of the Yorkshire Wildlife Trust, in protecting and managing valuable sites of nature conservation throughout this large and diverse county is there for all to see and appreciate.

This does not come cheaply both in terms of capital expenditure and running costs, and so the Trust is constantly looking at ways of raising the necessary finance to carry out its obligation effectively.

It was therefore, with great enthusiasm, that I welcomed this novel proposal by Judith Bromley to produce this book. I congratulate her on her determination in seeing the project through to its conclusion, and on her great skills in producing something so special, which I'm sure will be appreciated and enjoyed by many.

I wish the Book every success, particularly coming as it does in the 50th anniversary of the Trust.

Foreword

Over a period of fourteen years I was very frequently in Yorkshire, filming, often in Askrigg where once, leaning on a drystone wall and gazing at a meadow full of flowers, I met the author and artist of the book. 'Where are you going?' I asked; "to paint"; 'paint what?' "wildflowers at the bottom of this buttercup field"', she said. Perhaps it was to paint one of the pictures in these pages.

During those years I became intimately acquainted (since filming is a slow process) with a hillside here, a field there, a beck-side meadow or a stretch of woodland hiding myriad wild plants, and sometimes thought with a certain regret of my father's little spongebag filled with wet moss and kept in a poacher's pocket, into which he would carefully insert varieties of tiny wildflowers that he thought rare or unusual in their place, to bear them home and foster them.

This lovely collection of paintings reminds me of much that I miss now I am not so often in Yorkshire; and of the years of my youth when meadows rich in wildflowers were safe from the sprays and the industrial developments of modern farming. Somehow we must try to ensure that the beauty of nature's miniatures is not only remembered, but preserved in its small glory.

Robert Hardy

'96

I spent a good deal of my childhood living in rural North Yorkshire, and grew up feeling "at one" with the countryside around me. I was particularly drawn to the wild flowers, learned their local names, and regarded them as friends to look for and greet as they re-appeared each year.

Having subsequently lived in the cities of Leeds and London, where large parks surrounded by buildings served as country for me, coming to live and work in the Yorkshire Dales was like coming home. I'm lucky to be able to make a living out of what I've always loved to do: roaming the hills and fields, exploring the riverside, wandering through the woods.

In good weather I make studies of flowers and landscapes to use for my own reference indoors. Having discovered that this particular meadow was the best place to go to find many of the species, I began to visit often, and spend a great deal of time there - with the farmer's permission of course. I often write down my feelings and experiences when I'm out and about, this helps to conjure up the mood of the moment when I'm working on my paintings later.

This book is a collection of studies and written notes which were originally for my own use, I hope that sharing them in this way will give you a little of the pleasure I have gained by being in the meadow.

The way in to the field is through the stile, the dog is my companion and protector

January

During the blizzard, the wind whipped the snow into great drifts, stouring over the walls. After this there were days and days of grey calm. Slight powderings of snow came down almost continuously from a heavy sky.

Suddenly after all these dowly days, I woke to find the sun rising into a perfect sky, clear from horizon to horizon. Down in the meadow, where the floods had previously knocked down the walls, the storm has formed deep drifts. The snow lies in long, sweeping curves, and is puffed through the walls in thick cushioned lumps. Hoar frost clings to everything: dead seed heads, branches, twigs, wire fences. During the night, thin pieces of ice have crept over the surface of the river, which now gently steams in the morning sun, and the still air.

Trees bare of leaves allow distant views of soft white hills from which the melt will descend to rejuvenate the water meadows.

Footprints in the snow bear witness of a bustling wildlife, the countryside is not asleep. Mosses and liverworts abound, the slightest breath of spring stirring them to complete cycles of life to produce stalked capsules replete with spores. And there safe beneath the soil tilled by prying frosts and the burrowing of earthworms are bulbs, corms, rhizomes and of course seeds, waiting to gild the fields with myriad flowers and butterflies. Would the ninety eight percent of our meadows lost in the last fifty years bloom again.

February

The weather held January's ice and snow in a severe grip
for weeks. Nothing appeared to change much in the meadow

Just when I had begun to believe that it would never be any different
there was a very sudden thaw. The wind changed from the east
which brings the snow, to the west, which is often milder.

One day of drizzly murk was followed by a day of clear sun
and warmth. Snow melted so quickly that the river flooded
for the second time this winter, bringing down the precious
goodness to the meadow. I waded through thick mud to get
here, but down by the river I realise that the silt the flood
brings is of quite a different quality to the soil of the fields
further back. It is sandy, and has piled up into
drifts, like the snow it replaced.

The sun dazzles brightly on the floodwater.
From west to east, the meadow is
combed into wavy
lines by wind
and water.

It looks totally devastated, littered with piles of driftwood and rubbish - gone are the pretty seedheads and dried grasses. It's hard to believe, seeing it in this state, that it is just this dereliction which makes the meadow so special for the spring and summer flowers. Looking carefully I can see bright red, and pale green, and yellow-white points pushing from the flattened earth, upwards into the warming air.

March

There is still snow on the hills, and the
meadow is littered with driftwood from so
many floods. Cold winds have held back the spring

The pussy willow buds are just beginning to swell
and leaves and shoots are pushing up
through the winter rubbish.

I can identify sweet cicely, burnet, and dog's mercury
among the other patterns and shapes which are
beginning to form a fresh carpet underfoot.

The air is filled with the choruses of sheep and lambs
and the twitterings and bubblings of
skylarks and curlew.
A pair of ducks fly off the river.

A celandine opens in the weak sun, and
pungent green shafts of garlic push
through the earth under the trees.

A clump of snowdrops has come into flower
the bulbs were probably swept downstream
from a garden years ago, whilst
the river was in spate.

Fertile silt surrenders up new growths,
red curled points of bistort,
fat purple shoots of butterbur,
and a mass of soft
forget-me-not leaves
by the bankside.

Pussy
Willow
salix sp.

Snowdrop
galanthus
nivalis

Celandine
ranunculus ficaria

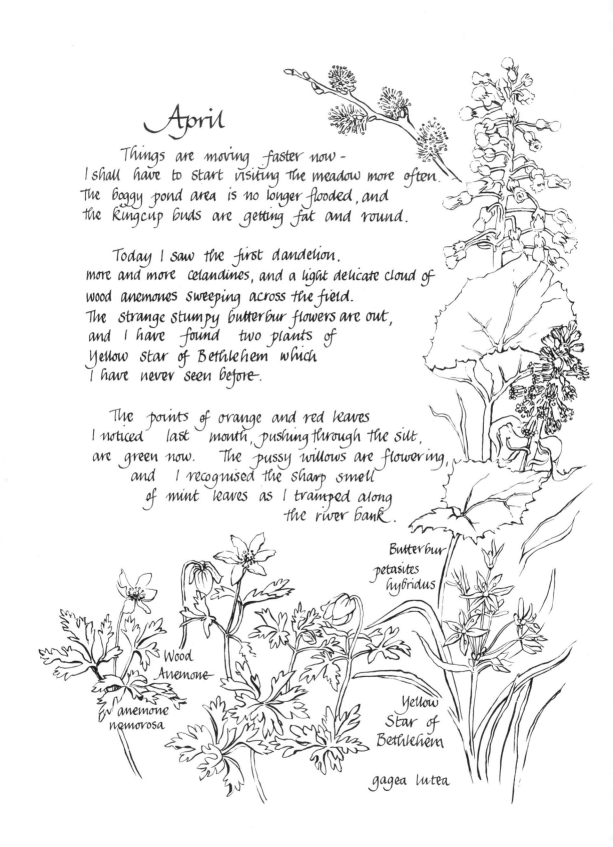

April

Things are moving faster now —
I shall have to start visiting the meadow more often.
The boggy pond area is no longer flooded, and
the kingcup buds are getting fat and round.

Today I saw the first dandelion.
more and more celandines, and a light delicate cloud of
wood anemones sweeping across the field.
The strange stumpy butterbur flowers are out,
and I have found two plants of
Yellow Star of Bethlehem which
I have never seen before.

The points of orange and red leaves
I noticed last month, pushing through the silt,
are green now. The pussy willows are flowering,
and I recognised the sharp smell
of mint leaves as I tramped along
the river bank.

Butterbur
petasites
hybridus

Wood
Anemone

anemone
nemorosa

Yellow
Star of
Bethlehem

gagea lutea

Curlew time is the sign that Spring has really arrived, along with the new lambs, and it seems as if the countryside turns green overnight. The clarion call of the curlew epitomises the sense of hope which comes with the onset of Spring. Seeing the world come alive again at this time of year is a real tonic and the fact that it happens every year, without any effort on our part, does not make it any the less special.

Judi Dench

CURLEW TIME

Early May

Everything changes rapidly
between each visit. The wood anemones
are still sparkling in the greening green.
The rose bush which was stark and empty,
now bears bunches of carefully folded leaves.

The driftwood has been collected into piles, ready for
removing: it could cause havoc with the haytime machines.

Yellow bursts of dandelions look to the sun, and early
milkmaids stand daintily where the grass grows longer.
A group of lambs have trespassed from a
nearby field and are steadily munching their
way through the new flavours.

The pond is drying up, but kingcups, growing
lusciously, show where the soil is still damp.
A curlew steps delicately. It has seen me and
is calling, but not flying off. There must be
something good to eat there, for it's probing
the soil only feet away from me....

Walking on, I've nearly stepped on its nest:
so that's what it was doing.
drawing my attention from four
speckled eggs in a slight
hollow

Kingcup
caltha
palustris

Dogs Mercury
Murcuralis
Perennis

Dandelion
taraxacum
officinale

Crosswort
Galium
Cruciata

Greater
Stitchwort
Stellaria
holostea

Lady's mantle
Alchemilia
vulgaris

Mid May

There is a warmth
in the gentle misty morning
and I walked straight to
the river where the sight of the
female butterbur took my breath away.
It stands high and proud, with all its seedheads
open like dandelion clocks, the sun shining
through both them and the mist.
The leaves of the butterbur are
broadening into those flat umberellas
the children love in summer.

Ramsons - wild garlic - spear upward,
flowers still wrapped in green sheaths,
out of a lush tangle of different
patterns and textures of leaves.
The earthnut, or pignut, is showing,
though still tightly curled.

Along the wall by the big tree, I have
found primroses, violets, cowslips, and
Soldiers buttons, with the stitchwort
twinkling white stars everywhere:
and then. the joy of finding a group of
early purple orchids! - such
a vivid colour in the
velvet green.

Sorrel
rumex
acetosa

Milkmaid
Cardamine
pratensis

Earthnut
conopodium
majus

Early Purple
Orchid
orchis mascula

Buttercup

ranunculus
bulbosus

Soldiers
Buttons
geum
rivale

Cowslip

primula
veris

Primrose
primula
vulgaris

Violet
viola riviniana

To read this evocation of Yorkshire is to bring back the sights and sounds of my childhood.

I was brought up in Dewsbury, among the dark satanic mills of a typical West Riding mill town, but the glory of Yorkshire is that the countryside is never far away.

I had never heard of artificial fertilisers as a girl. Certainly the wild flowers which I remember suggest that they were not yet used on a large scale.

Late May, through June to haymaking, was always a wonderful time in my native county, particularly when we travelled afield to the Dales. This book, with its illustrations, recalls it all so well.

Speaker

BUTTERCUP FIELD

Early June

I have walked, through
fields of growing grass scattered
with flowers, to the stile leading into
the meadow. By this time, many of the other
fields have been treated with artificial
fertilisers, which encourage certain grasses to
take over from the other herbs.
This field relies on the river-flooding, and
upon the manure from grazing stock, to enrich
its soil. It is never sprayed. So the wild flowers
are left to flourish naturally.
The colour over the wall is almost dazzling.
Stepping through the stile is like stepping into magic.
The field is a bobbing plain of yellow buttercups,
interspersed with the brilliant purple and magenta
of wood cranesbills, white of earthnut,
and brown and cream of plantain.
The curlews curse at me again, calling shrilly in
the clear air. The edge of the meadow is a creamy
foam of sweet cicely growing luxuriantly,
smelling of aniseed, lapping the permeter
of the sparkling, brightly studded
field ... vetch, campion, stitchwort,
water avens, red clover, and
ramsons · the names themselves
ring with colour and
variety.....

Bistort
polygonum
bistorta

Plantain
plantago
lanceolata

Buttercup
ranunculus
acris

Clover
trifolium
pratense

Wood Cranesbill
geranium
sylvaticum

... I wandered round, not wanting to miss anything, choosing a place to sit. I found mint and garlic growing savoury together. Cow parsley floats, white and green, above the butterbur umberellas. Pigeons are nesting in the willows, skylarks bubble, and black swifts arrow past, skimming over the sea of colour. Pink patches of bistort stand tall where those points of red and orange were only weeks ago, and in some places the earthnut and cow parsley predominate - but the whole meadow warms and glistens with buttercup yellow. The gentle wind makes waves of pink, yellow, green and white.

The sun is warm; birds burble and sing;
  insects buzz busily in the fragrant
    cups of colour.
      The buttercups try
        to face the
        sun - but the wind
        blows them back
        to face me as I sit
      and paint. The dog's
    black face is dusted with pollen
  as she sleeps beneath the budding
hawthorn - little round creamy buds
bursting into starry blossoms of white.
  I've never realised before how
      quickly one species takes
          over from another,
            influencing the
                overall colour of
                  the field.

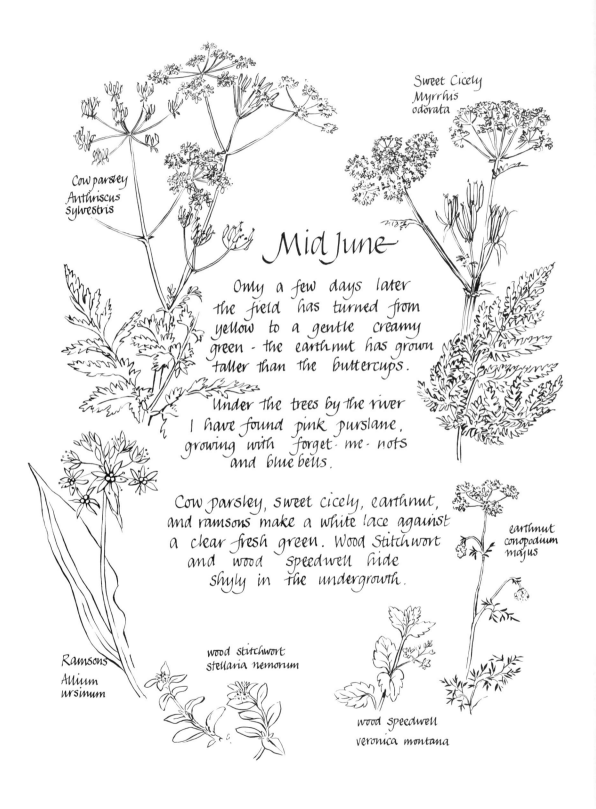

Cow parsley
Anthriscus
sylvestris

Sweet Cicely
Myrrhis
odorata

Mid June

Only a few days later
the field has turned from
yellow to a gentle creamy
green - the earthnut has grown
taller than the buttercups.

Under the trees by the river
I have found pink purslane,
growing with forget-me-nots
and bluebells.

Cow parsley, sweet cicely, earthnut,
and ramsons make a white lace against
a clear fresh green. Wood Stitchwort
and wood speedwell hide
shyly in the undergrowth.

earthnut
conopodium
majus

Ramsons
Allium
ursinum

wood stitchwort
stellaria nemorum

wood speedwell
veronica montana

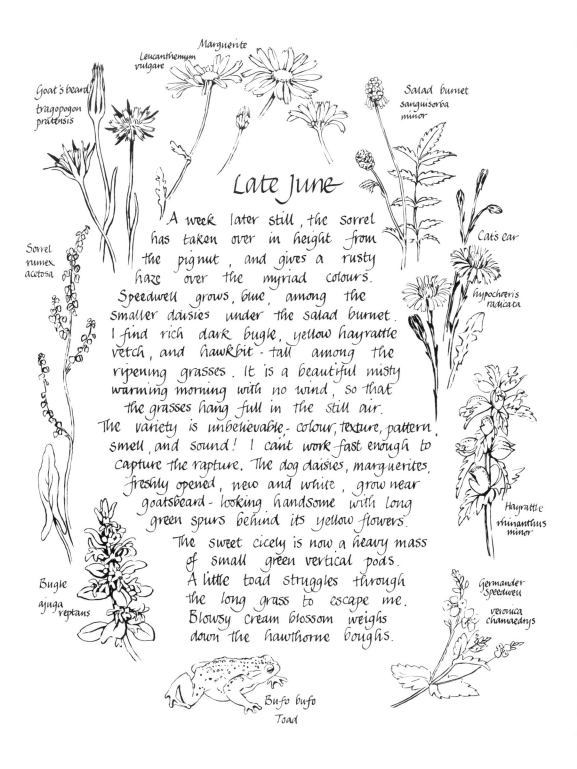

Marguerite
Leucanthemum vulgare

Goat's beard
tragopogon pratensis

Salad burnet
sanguisorba minor

Cat's ear

Sorrel
rumex acetosa

hypochoeris radicata

Late June

A week later still, the sorrel has taken over in height from the pignut, and gives a rusty haze over the myriad colours. Speedwell grows, blue, among the smaller daisies under the salad burnet. I find rich dark bugle, yellow hayrattle vetch, and hawkbit - tall among the ripening grasses. It is a beautiful misty warming morning with no wind, so that the grasses hang full in the still air. The variety is unbelievable - colour, texture, pattern, smell, and sound! I can't work fast enough to capture the rapture. The dog daisies, marguerites, freshly opened, new and white, grow near goatsbeard - looking handsome with long green spurs behind its yellow flowers.

The sweet cicely is now a heavy mass of small green vertical pods. A little toad struggles through the long grass to escape me. Blowsy cream blossom weighs down the hawthorne boughs.

Hayrattle
rhinanthus minor

Bugle
ajuga reptans

Germander Speedwell
veronica chamaedrys

Bufo bufo
Toad

Hawkbit
leontodon autumnalis

Tufted Vetch
vicia cracca

Birdsfoot Trefoil
lotus
corniculatus

White Clover
trifolium repens

Self Heal
prunella vulgaris

Common Spotted Orchis
dactylorhiza fuchsii

Early July

The weather is marvellous,
hot and sunny with a light breeze.
The fields around buzz with tractors,
busy cutting, turning and gathering grass
Some of the fields were cut earlier for
silage, but the weather is so good, a few
farmers have now started haytiming.

I sit by the river in the heat and calm,
surrounded by daisies, hawkbits, birdsfoot trefoil,
clovers, self heal, vetches, and the pollen-
heavy grasses. Some common spotted orchids
have appeared by the bank, and the
purple tufted vetch is a mass of colour.

It is difficult to sit and paint
without squashing something, but the
farmer has given me permission,
and, with care of course, to walk
around the outside where I find
huge melancholy thistles.

In my junior school days after school and tea there was still time and light in high summer to go walking in the fields around home with my friends before cricket became my favourite pastime. I remember lots of wild flowers underfoot, many of which I couldn't put a name to, but just as familiar as the hayricks when the hay was cut. Strange how you take some things in nature for granted, only to find they have disappeared.

Geoff
Boycott.

The field is cut.
I went away for a few days, and when I
returned I found a note on my
kitchen table to say that they
were cutting it. That was yesterday.

The fresh cut grass and flowers lie in flat, broad lines, curving to the shape
of the field. Still standing round the edge is a fair selection of what
lies cut in the middle; purple tufted vetch, daisies and buttercups;
knapweed heads are still hard round buds, hence their local
name - 'hardheads'; bush vetch climbs more secretly among
the grass; there is great burnet, meadow vetchling,
germander speedwell, crosswort, hogweed, and hawkbit;
ragwort is just peeping out, with meadowsweet unfolding;
yarrow has open flat white dishes of flowers, hay rattle with
purpling seedboxes lies with the yellow birdsfoot trefoil;
lesser stitchwort still twinkles among the green patterns of leaves,
a more mature green now, than its earlier freshness. ....

Dog Rose
rosa canina

.... Clover, growing tall, is supported by
lush grasses, next to the thistles, which
have tight folded buds. Soft pink grass bends
in the wind, or lies cut on flat dry ground.
Tall delicate grass heads gently shimmer
against the rough, lichen-textured wall.
Nettles stand high, holding reddish and cream
flower clusters at the base of their leaf stalks.
Sweet cicely seedheads are swelling ochre and olive spikes
in their frill of lacy leaves. A campion stands, proud and bright,
pink yarrow heads glow against the blue green lichen.

The noise of bees and busy tractors fills the air- hurrying
whilst the weather lasts. It's early to cut this field, but
very dry, and many of the flowers had faded. I hope
the seeds have done their job- spreading a
promise for next year, but the roots are still
there, making sure of a return. I've heard it
said that a farmer may avoid paying large vet's
bills by feeding his stock on hay like this-
some of the herbs either preventing or curing
sicknesses before they become a problem.

The wild rose bushes are blooming, pink and white,
St John's wort grows at the top of the bank, and
self heal, less boldly, among the grass at
the bottom. Meadow cranesbill,
bluer than its smaller relative is
growing in the wall near the pond.

Red Campion
silene dioica

Forgetme·not
myosotis
scorpioides

Goosegrass
galium aparine

.... The high grasses near the pond
have opened out now and hang tall
and graceful. A dock growing against the
grass is gently changing colour from yellow-green
to red. A melancholy thistle has taken root here,
"melancholy" seems quite the wrong name for
such a huge, purple velvet cushion.

The overgrown "rubbish" end near the ford
remains uncut. lesser willow herb, struggling
for space among huge hogweed, butterbur leaves
and six foot grasses. Across this jungle I can see
a great bellflower spike coming up, tall and pale.
It's hard to walk through all this to the dry
river, where forget·me·nots, blue and lush, hang
over shiny green stones, next to a patch of
brooklime with its deeper blue and shiny leaves.
Pink purslane, still flowering. hides under the
river bank, on which grow chickweed and
goosegrass. A family of moorhens are
angry at my presence and make warning
calls to chicks, who run for cover....

Pink
Persicaria
polygonum
persicaria

Spearmint
mentha
spicata

Lesser
Willow Herb

epilobium
parviflorum

Brooklime
veronica
becca bunga

Pink Purslane
montia sibirica

.... Humming tractors turn and collect
dry hay, while in the low, slow
river, trout leap and plop back
into the water, teasing the
dog who tries to chase them.

A goats·beard, which had stubbornly
refused to open its seedhead when I
wanted to paint it, is now lying
cut with the orchids in the hay,
and has fully opened its beautiful
round clock of feathery seeds.
I managed to capture it before the
breeze blew the will-o'-the-wisp
tops up and away.
The field was cut right up to
the river bank, but creamy
meadowsweet, daisies, dark blue
vetch, meadow vetchling, purple
thistle and figwort grow on a
piece which has broken off from
the main bank. A bunch of
bladder campion hangs there too,
beginning to shrivel in the dry weather.
The flat, empty field, cleared of hay,
is still bleaching out
and prickly. The
figwort glistens, and
a meadow vetchling
among a patch of
long grass, climbs
higher and
higher.

Figwort   Scrophularia
nodosa

Bladder Campion
silene vulgaris

Bush Vetch
vicia sepium

We would always head for North Yorkshire at the weekends. I don't even know where really, we would just cross the Pennines and head upwards, my father's estate car straining in low gear. I seem to remember one of his cars was a Singer, or am I mixing it up with my mother's sewing machine?

We didn't do much when we got there, mainly sit staring through the windscreen while my father brewed up. It took me a long time to realise landscapes looked better without two windscreen wipers.

I'm a bit of a walker now. I even have a bobble hat. Sometimes I wear two pairs of socks. Sometimes I dash up tracks in an aerobic buttock-toning way, but mainly I potter about with the children, staring over gates while they sing Baa Baa Black Sheep to puzzled ditto.

This summer I had an evening in a North Yorkshire garden. No children, no responsibilities, nothing to do but get myself on a plane the next morning. I just sat. It was very hot, and still. There was no wind and no sound apart from the little steam train chuffing back and forth at Embsay. I watched the sun go down over the rookery and the colour fade from the hills. A breather.

AFTERMATH

Late July

When haytiming had finished, and the farmers had held their "mell's", - the Dales equivalent of harvest suppers, the weather broke and is now wet and windy.

I'm not able to sit out and paint the flowers, which are swaying too much in the wind; but I enjoy the welcome moisture which revives the plants and brightens them up.

Meadow Vetchling
lathyrus pratensis

Horsetail
equisetum palustre

Melancholy
Thistle
circium
heterophyllum

Hogweed
heracleum
sphondylium

Greater
Bellflower
Campanula
latifolia

Early
August

As I approach a curlew runs
among the new green grass blades,
fresh and bright after the rain. The stile
is adorned with meadowsweet and
great burnet on one side, and thistles
and burdock on the other.
The plants and grasses now
have that "end-of-summer" look.

The knapweed is a vivid magenta, with
some blue-purple vetch and red campion against
a grey wall. The curlew still shouts at me as I
walk round the edge of the field. The yarrow is
huge and full, matching the flat white lichen patches
on the wall. Harebells crowd with meadowsweet, and the
stitchwort twinkles on. Many great bellflowers tower in the long
grass near the river, pale presences under the trees. Three mallard
rise from the water, where the aroma of mint sharpens the air.

Further away from the trees are wood woundwort, melancholy
thistles, and more of those bell spires, a deeper colour where there
is more light. Hogweed seedheads battle skywards with
tall grasses, blond and dry now, and taller than them all.

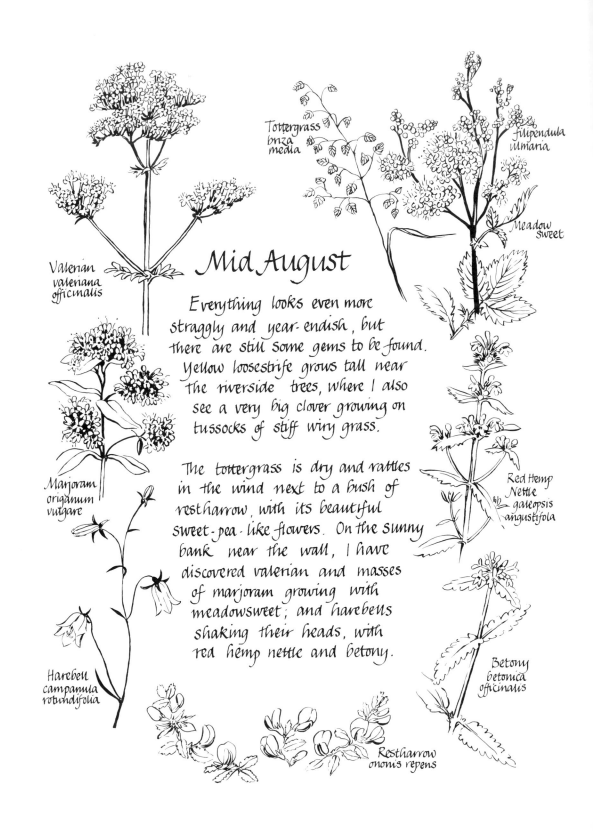

Tottergrass
briza
media

filipendula
ulmaria

Meadow
sweet

Valerian
valeriana
officinalis

Mid August

Everything looks even more
straggly and year-endish, but
there are still some gems to be found.
Yellow loosestrife grows tall near
the riverside trees, where I also
see a very big clover growing on
tussocks of stiff wiry grass.

The tottergrass is dry and rattles
in the wind next to a bush of
restharrow, with its beautiful
sweet-pea-like flowers. On the sunny
bank near the wall, I have
discovered valerian and masses
of marjoram growing with
meadowsweet; and harebells
shaking their heads, with
red hemp nettle and betony.

Marjoram
origanum
vulgare

Red Hemp
Nettle
galeopsis
angustifola

Harebell
campanula
rotundifolia

Betony
betonica
officinalis

Restharrow
ononis repens

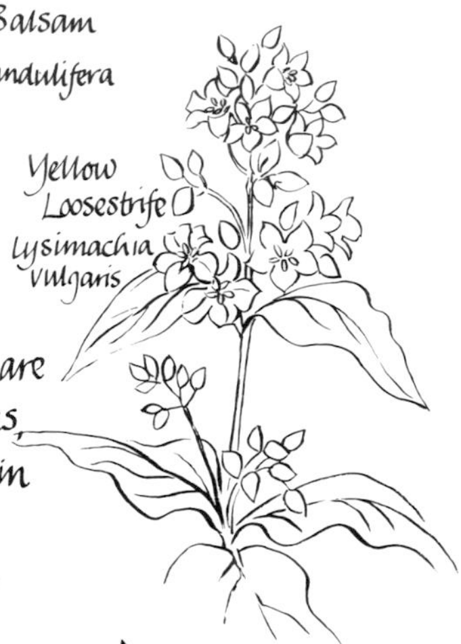

Indian Balsam
impatiens glandulifera

Hawkweed hieracium agg.

Yellow
Loosestrife
lysimachia
vulgaris

.... The meadow cranesbills are
a beautiful blue, white scabious,
paler heads on long stalks, wave in
the breeze by the river bank.
Yellow Autumn hawkbit continues
the dandelion-like theme through
to the end of the year, together with
another very tall hawkweed
growing under the trees.

Scabious
knautia
arvensis

By the river are a few
monkey flowers, known
locally as monkey musk,
velvety with red spots at its throat.

Meadow
Cranesbill
geranium
pratense

Indian Balsam encroaches higher
up the river each year, a
persistent "offcumden"
which could take
over everything.
Pink persicaria
struggles among it
in the rough end
of the field.

Field
Garlic
allium
oleracium

Monkey Musk

mimulus
gutatus

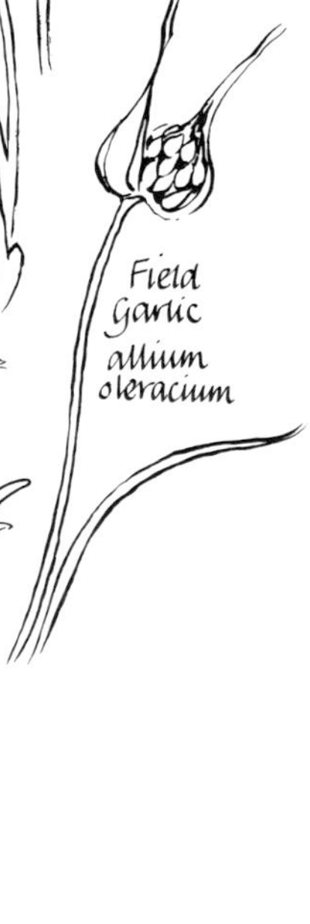

Autumn
Hawkbit
leontodon autumnalis

September

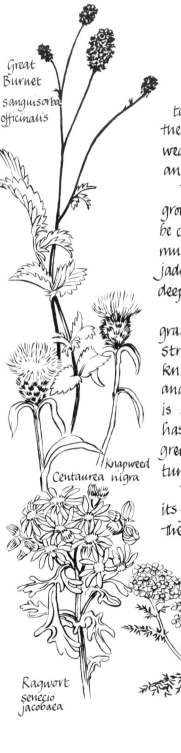

Great Burnet
sanguisorba officinalis

Knapweed
Centaurea nigra

Ragwort
senecio jacobaea

Yarrow
achillea millefolium

Summer has ended with a massive storm - the tail end of a hurricane. The river flooded and the wind smashed down the taller plants. If the weather brightens now, it will be for a fine autumn, an Indian summer.

The fog, or follow-on-grass after the hay is cut, has grown quite lush, but the storm ruined it before it could be cut for a second crop. It is very green because of so much rain, and the odd flower perks up amid a sea of jade: cerise wood cranesbill, white dog daisy, pink bistort, deep red great burnet and yellow autumn hawkbit.

Butterbur leaves are old and battered, with dry grasses and tobacco brown seed clusters of sweet cicely straggling along the riverside. Yellow ragwort and knapweed still doggedly flower on in the cooling air and shortening days. That huge patch of forget-me-nots is still blooming, but its neighbour, the brooklime has finished. The leaves on the trees are a darkening green, except for on one small sycamore, where they've turned yellow and started to fall.

The Indian balsam has got to the 'fun' stage, when its pendulous heavy seed pods burst energetically at the slightest touch, shooting the seeds far and wide. I hope it doesn't take over from the native hogweed, bellflower, loosestrife, tall stately dock and sweet cicely. It can bully them out of existence with its virility.

The pond is full again. The sunny bank is still a mass of knapweed and marjoram, with a little meadowsweet, and a few late harebells.

October

We have got our Indian summer. days of clear skies and warm sun. just what we need to prepare us for a hard winter. The thistles have been beautiful with their fluffy seed tops opening in the sun. Today I found the stile framed by them, the prickly lichen walls stuck with soft gossamer.

The trees are all at different stages - some still green, others warming to yellows, oranges, and browns, and one or two quite bare.

Young black and white cattle break off from grazing to lumber friskily after the dog who dashes back to the stile and waits there for me.

I think of the year as beginning in autumn; that was when one went to a new school or went up a class; it was when I went off to university. I even went into the army in August so the back-end always seems to me the time for new beginnings.

Not much liking the heat I'm always glad to see the back of summer and though I enjoy warm October days I'm happy that the sun has lost its power. Also the back-end means one can go walking with a purpose. There's blackberrying, which I was brought up to do as a child in Leeds during the war, though one couldn't get far in those days so blackberries were much sought after. There was one field in East Keswick near Harewood where there'd often be two dozen hikers scouring the bushes (or 'blegging' as my Dad called it).

Mushrooming is another autumn pleasure, the almost luminous glow of a horse mushroom in a green field never fails to cheer me. I go back to the same fields year after year; haphazard and unpredictable, the occurrence of mushrooms always a mystery and a surprise.

Alan Bennett

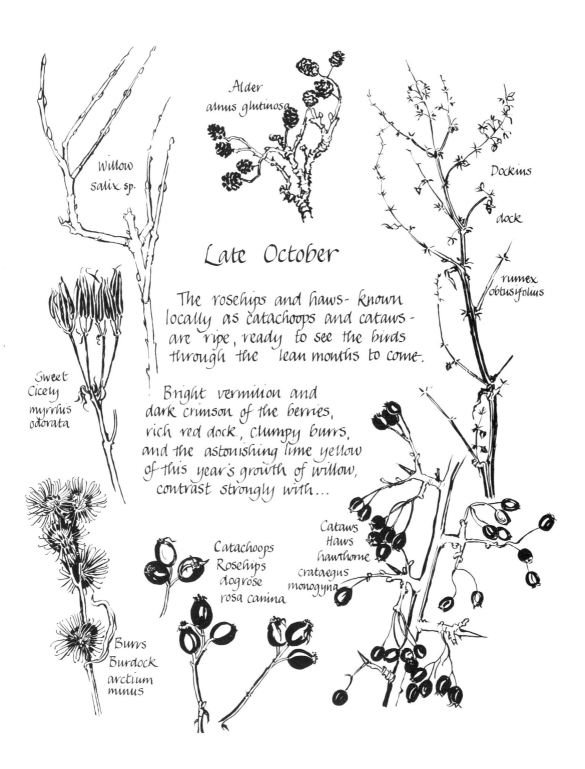

Willow
salix sp.

Alder
alnus glutinosa

Dockins

dock

rumex
obtusifolius

Late October

The rosehips and haws- known
locally as catachoops and cataws -
are ripe, ready to see the birds
through the lean months to come.

Bright vermilion and
dark crimson of the berries,
rich red dock, clumpy burrs,
and the astonishing lime yellow
of this year's growth of willow,
contrast strongly with...

Sweet
Cicely
myrrhis
odorata

Catachoops
Rosehips
dogrose
rosa canina

Cataws
Haws
hawthorne
crataegus
monogyna

Burrs
Burdock
arctium
minus

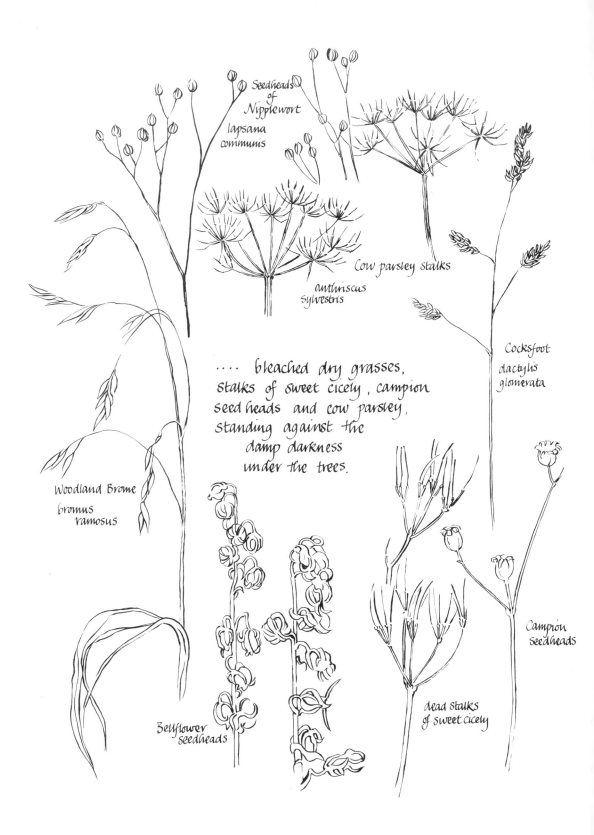

Seedheads
of
Nipplewort
lapsana
communis

Cow parsley stalks

anthriscus
sylvestris

Cocksfoot
dactylis
glomerata

.... bleached dry grasses,
stalks of sweet cicely, campion
seed heads and cow parsley,
standing against the
damp darkness
under the trees.

Woodland Brome
bromus
ramosus

Bellflower
seedheads

dead stalks
of sweet cicely

Campion
seedheads

November

Today is a misty, dowly day, but
as I walk around, the sun comes
through, silhouetting the bleak

trees against the soft blanket of fog, and making
the lichen glow brilliantly on the walls. The lichen
and moss are at their best in this damp weather,
jewel colours on the grey stones. The fog turns
soft primrose where the sun shines through it.

December

Very bad floods
have swept over
everything, knocking down
walls and fences. Twigs, branches,
old grasses, are all left clinging
to those walls and trees which
remain upright. All the longer
grass is flattened and shows where
the current swept, strongly curving
around objects in its path.
The areas of abandoned
floodwater are now frozen.
Sharp patterns and beautiful curves in
the ice show where it got colder in stages.
Short tufts of grass stick up near great piles of frozen debris

The year is at an end, with very little sign of life anywhere.

Wildflowers found in the Hay Meadow

SCIENTIFIC NAME	ENGLISH NAME	LOCAL NAME
Achillea millefolium	Yarrow	
Ajuga reptans	Bugle	
Alchemilla glabra	Lady's mantle	
A. xanthochlora	Lady's mantle	
Alliaria petiolata	Garlic mustard	Jack-by-the-hedge
Allium oleraceum	Field garlic	
A. ursinium	Ramsons, wild garlic	Ramps
Anemone nemorosa	Wood anemone	
Angelica sylvestris	Wild angelica	
Anthriscus sylvestris	Cow parsley	Keck, kexies
Arctium minus	Burdock	Burrs
Aster sp.	Michaelmas daisy	
Bellis perennis	Daisy	
Brassica oleracea x rapa	Wild turnip	
Caltha palustris	Marsh marigold	Kingcups
Calystegia sepium	Bindweed	
Campanula latifolia	Giant bellflower	Canterbury bell
C. rotundifolia	Harebell	
Cardamine amara	Large bittercress	
C. flexuosa	Wavy bittercress	
C. pratensis	Lady's smock	Cuckoo flower, milkmaids
Centuarea nigra	Knapweed	Hardheads
Cerastium holosteoides	Chickweed	Mouse-ear
Cirsium arvense	Creeping thistle	
C. heterophyllum	Melancholy thistle	
C. vulgare	Spear thistle	
Conopodium majus	Earthnut	Pignut
Crataegus monogyna	Common hawthorn	Cataws
Crepis capillaris	Smooth hawksbeard	
Dactylorhiza fuchsii	Common spotted orchid	
Epilobium parriflorum	Hairy willow herb	
Endymion non-scriptus	Bluebell	
Equisetum arvense	Field horsetail	
Filipendula ulmaria	Meadowsweet	
F. vulgaris	Dropwort	
Gagea lutea	Yellow Star of Bethlehem	
Galanthus nivalis	Snowdrop	

Galeopsis angustifolia	Red hemp nettle	
Galium aparine	Goosegrass	Sweethearts
G. cruciata	Crosswort	
G. verum	Lady's bedstraw	
Geranium pratense	Meadow cranesbill	
G.sylvaticum	Wood cranesbill	
Geum rivale	Water avens	Soldier's buttons
G. urbanum	Wood avens	Herb bennet
Heracleum sphondylium	Hogweed	
Hieracium agg.	Hawkweed	
Hypericum hirsutum	Hairy St. John's wort	
Hypochoeris radicata	Cat's ear	
Impatiens glandulifera	Indian balsam	Policeman's helmet
Knautia arvensis	Field Scabious	
Lamium album	White deadnettle	
Lapsana communis	Nipplewort	
Lathyrus pratensis	Meadow vetchling	
Leontodon autumnalis	Autumn hawkbit	
L. hispidus	Rough hawkbit	
Leucanthemum vulgare	Ox-eye daisy	Dog daisy, marguerite
Lotus corniculatus	Birdsfoot trefoil	Bacon & eggs
L. uliginosus	Greater birdsfoot trefoil	
Lysimachia vulgaris	Yellow loosestrife	
Mercurialis perennis	Dogs Mercury	
Mentha spicata	Spearmint	
Mimulus guttatus	Monkey flower	Monkey musk
Montia sibirica	Pink purslane	
Myosotis arvensis	Common forget-me-not	
M. discolor	Yellow forget-me-not	
M. scorpioides	Water forget-me-not	
Myrrhis odorata	Sweet cicely	Aniseed
Ononis repens	Restharrow	
Orchis mascula	Early purple orchid	
Origanum vulgare	Marjoram	
Petasites hybridus	Butterbur	
Plantago lanceolata	Ribwort plantain	
Polygonum bistorta	Common bistort	Snakeweed
P. persicaria	Pink persicaria	
Potentilla sterilis	Barren strawberry	
Primula veris	Cowslip	

P. vulgaris	Primrose	
Prunella vulgaris	Self-heal	
Ranunculus acris	Meadow buttercup	
R. bulbosus	Bulbous buttercup	
R. ficaria	Lesser celandine	
R. repens	Creeping buttercup	
Rhinanthus minor	Yellow rattle	Hay rattle
Roripa sp.	Yellow cress	
Rosa canina	Dog rose	Hips-catachoops
Rumex acetosa	Common sorrel	
R. obtusifolius	Broad-leaved dock	Dockins
Salix sp.	Pussy willow	Palms
Sanguisorba minor	Salad burnet	
S. officinalis	Greater burnet	
Scrophularia nodosa	Common figwort	
Senecio jacobea	Common ragwort	Dog standard, dog-banner
Silene dioica	Red campion	
S. vulgaris	Bladder campion	
Stachys officinalis (Betonica officinalis)	Betony	
S. sylvatica	Hedge woundwood	
Stellaria alsine	Bog stitchwort	
S. graminea	Lesser stitchwort	
S. holostea	Greater stitchwort	
S. nemorum	Wood stitchwort	
Taraxacum officinale	Dandelion	
Tragopogon pratensis	Goatsbeard	
Trifolium medium	Zigzag clover	
T. pratense	Red clover	
T. repens	White clover	
Urtica dioica	Stinging nettle	
Valeriana officinalis	Common valerian	
Veronica beccabunga	Brooklime	
V. chamaedrys	Germander speedwell	Birdseye
V. montana	Wood speedwell	
V. persica	Common field speedwell	
V. polita	Grey speedwell	
V. serpyllifolia	Thyme-leaved speedwell	
Vicia cracca	Tufted vetch	
V. sepium	Bush vetch	
Viola riviniana	Common dog violet	

Grasses, Sedges and Rushes of the Hay Meadow

SCIENTIFIC NAME	ENGLISH NAME	LOCAL NAME
Agrostis capilaris	Common bent	
Alopecurus pratensis	Meadow foxtail	
Anthoxanthum odoratum	Sweet vernal grass	
Arrhenatherum elatius	False oat grass	
Avenula pratense	Meadow oat grass	
A. pubescens	Downy oat grass	
Briza media	Quaking grass	Rattles, tottergrass
Bromus hordaceus	Soft brome	
B. ramosus	Hairy brome	
Carex acutiformis	Lesser pond sedge	
C. nigra	Common sedge	
Dactylis glomerata	Cocksfoot	
Deschampsia caespitosa	Tufted hair grass	
Festuca rubra	Red fescue	
Holcus lanatus	Yorkshire fog	
H. mollis	Creeping soft grass	
Lolium perenne	Perennial rye grass	
Luzula campestris	Field woodrush	
Phalaris arundinacea	Reed canary grass	
Poa pratensis	Smooth-stalked meadow grass	
P. trivialis	Rough-stalked meadow grass	
Trisetum flavescens	Yellow oat grass